A SIX
FIGURE
VISION

Tips to Making More Money Happiness and Success

Taurea Vision Avant

This book is dedicated to:

Beverly Melissa Doman Avant, my mother: the woman who taught me even at a very young age to push through challenges even when it may not seem like you'll make it.

Veronica Terry, my 2nd mother: the woman who taught me to not take everything so seriously, how to get over things that have no major impact on my life and how to have true patience. I love you with all my heart. Thank you for being my everything.

And, to **Andra Bernard Avant**, my father; the man who taught me to NEVER GIVE UP! You are where I learned how to have thick skin. x

Make Sure to Follow

Taurea Vision Avant on Social Media

@VisionAvant

Table of Contents

Acknowledgements

There are just so many people that I would like to thank who have had a major impact in my life. I would hate to leave anybody out. For anyone in my life that has been a friend through any challenge I've ever had, I want to thank you so very much. I can't name you all, but you know exactly who you are! I love you with all my heart.

When it comes to my personal development and growth, there are some people that I don't have a personal relationship with, but from afar they have helped me tremendously. These are all the women and men who are changing the world for the better. I would recommend that you follow them as well. Darren Hardy, Dani Johnson, Lisa Nicole Cloud, Lisa Nichols, Lisa Sasevich, Les Brown, Oprah Winfrey, Rhonda Byrne, Sara Blakely, Anthony Robbins, John C Maxwell, Jim Rohn, Bob Proctor, and France P. Martin. There are more, but make sure you also follow me, as I am always referring great reads on my website.

Also, there are some incredible visionaries that I would like to recognize with this 2nd edition. These are business owners that I have had the pleasure to be connected with. Many of them are in businesses that you can also join them or learn more directly from them. They are mentioned in the chapter on Making Multiple Streams of Income.

I also want to take time to say a special thanks to the visionaries who also supported this book before it was printed.

Alexis Ray a.ray@cheerful.com, **Amanda J Butler** ajbillionaire@gmail.com, **Andrella Pusha** apusha843@gmail.com, Jewel bijou777@comcast.net, **Joyce Brown** candifl@gmail.com, **Charisma DeZonie** cdezonie@gmail.com, **Constance Mckinsey Neal** cmneal1@gmail.com, **Annamaria Salley** Creditqueen811@gmail.com, **Cynthia Anderson** cynthiacanderson14@gmail.com, **DB Bedford** db.bedford@ineverworry.com, **Donna Thomas** donnathomas@cox.net, **Elissa Mitchell** Elissaiwillwork@gmail.com, **Lawrence Gantt** globalgrindmagazine@gmail.com, **Deseree Jabbar** Gracelivelife@gmail.com, **Chinyere Helyn Njoku** helynscorner@gmail.com, **Latiera Ford** info@authorlatieraford.com, **Orlando Haynes** Info@coupledforwealth.com, **Deric Robinson** info@digitalcometapps.com, **Teia Acker** Info@ebonyivoryps.com, **Lisa Stringer Bailey** ladybosslbailey@gmail.com, **Malika Tewari** Mtewaribrown@gmail.com, **Annette Bryant** OhenewaaTravel7@gmail.com, **Patricia Pearson** Pat@coachpatpearson.com, **Vivian Smith-Barnes** Queenviv@rocketmail.com, **Regina Kenan** reginakenan@gmail.com, **Elaine Bailey** roadofabundance@gmail.com, **Sonja Keeve** sakeeve40@gmail.com, **Shantell London** Shntlllamark@yahoo.com, **Tara Waggoner** tarawaggoner@gmail.com, **Stephanie Allen** thestephanieallen1@gmail.com and **Elissa Mitchell** youhavenoideabook@outlook.com

Introduction

Freedom... What does it mean to you? Do you know how to get? Have you made a decision that you are tired of not being able to do what you truly want to do? Then you have come to the right place.

A Six Figure Vision was written because I want to be able to reach people by helping them with the challenges that I've dealt with through life. I feel that our journey in life is not always about us, but also who we can help. Being able to live the type of life I live, some would only dream about. I don't mean living this life because of the clothes I wear or the car I drive; I believe that my life is amazing because I truly get to schedule my life according to how I want it. I hated the day when I had to ask my boss if I could go visit my father, who was sick. I wasn't able to spend time with him during his last months on Earth. I hated having to get permission to leave work early. I hated driving in traffic every single day. I hated not having money to go on the trips that I desired. Even though I loved myself, I hated a lot about how I was living my life. I believe that the reason why most people go through life hating things is because they just haven't been made aware. That's why I wrote this book. I believe that I have been given an amazing gift, and it's my passion to be able to give this gift of awareness to over 100,000,000 families worldwide. This book is just the start!

By the way did you know this book came with bonuses? YUP simply go to bonus.asixfigurevision.com to get them today!

ENJOY!

<u>Chapter 1: What Does Freedom Mean?</u>

"Freedom starts within your thoughts, and then through action, you get to decide what comes out!"

Taurea V. Avant

What does Freedom mean?

You will find in this book that there are a lot of ingredients to having true freedom, but the first step, really, is to identify what freedom means to you. I see so many people living their lives today without meaning. People just wake up and do the same routines every day, over and over and over and never really know why. If you ask most of them, they will just say, "That's life." However, when you desire to have true freedom, you must first identify what you want. To me, freedom means being able to do what I want to do, when I want to do it, with whom I want, and wherever I want. My idea of freedom means to be in state of peace. When I think of freedom, I see love, happiness and abundance. I remember being in a place where I did not know what freedom meant, and I also remember how it made me feel. When I finally made a decision on what I wanted out of life, things started to change immediately for me. Remember that freedom is available to anyone, and it's my goal to help you go after it!

In this chapter, I will briefly discuss some key elements in obtaining freedom. In the following chapters, I will be going in depth and breaking them all down.

Think about Freedom

Because I had decided that I would be free, my next step was to start thinking it. Every great creation first started with a thought. Everything in life had to be thought of first before it was even created. This is why our thoughts are so powerful. There are three types of thinking: conscious thinking, subconscious thinking, and unconscious thinking.

Conscious thinking is being aware of what you're thinking about. Conscious thought, when put simply, is being aware of what's going on in your mind. You control what you focus on. When you first learn to make a dish, you are consciously aware of what you are doing; measuring every ingredient, setting the right temperatures and then one day it becomes effortless.

Subconscious thinking is when things just become a part of your everyday life. You no longer have to think about it. For example, when you first learned to drive you were consciously thinking of what you were doing. After a while, driving became a part of your subconscious thinking. You start your car and take off. You even find yourself doing multiple things at once while driving. You don't have to think about braking, as it just becomes a part of your normal thought process.

Unconscious thinking can be better seen as the thinking that you do when you are asleep. Of course, you are unconsciously thinking at all times; however, it's my opinion that this is one of the most powerful because what you think of unconsciously is what truly forms your subconscious and your conscious thinking. Unconscious thinking is who you are. Our unconscious thinking controls our beliefs. It is the ability to perform tasks outside of being aware.

To change your life, you must first start with your conscious thinking, which will transform to your subconscious and finally the ultimate goal, which is to be at an unconscious freedom thought. You will learn how to do just that in this book.

To Speak is To Create

Now that you are aware of your thoughts, you must now acknowledge that your words are even more powerful. All ideas were first created with a thought, but they didn't go into creation until words were spoken. Millions of people believe that the world was created with words. However, even though people do believe that, many of them don't understand that there is a direct correlation to how important our words are. Be careful of what you speak because that is exactly what you will attract. I have students from all over the world, and one of the first things we work on is our words. If you want FREEDOM, you must speak freedom, and you must know what it means. Speak it daily and don't speak that of which you don't want in your life. It will be very hard at first, especially if you have never been aware of your speaking. However, when you learn to start working on your words, you will start to see that you will attract all of what you speak into your life.

The Future Depends on What You Do Today

The next step is to ACT. It is said that "faith without works is dead." "A goal without action is just a dream." Today, more people live with that lottery mentality. They want freedom, but most aren't willing to do what it takes. Think about it. The lottery is played by millions of people every single week; however, there are only a few winners. Why would we live our life like that—by just taking a chance on freedom? You are going to learn how to take the right activity steps in this book. I used to always dream of freedom, but I never really knew how to go and get it. I'm so grateful that I have been able to bless millions of families with the same opportunity I was given. My passion is to help you do the same. Activity is everything, and we are going to start taking steps today!

Freedom is About Choice

Now you have to make a choice that you really want this. What do I mean by making a choice? Well, you must understand that once you have identified the actions you are going to take, you must stay focused on that activity and not allow your focus to be broken. I always talk about having "broken focus." Most people who never obtain freedom also are known to be all over the place with their thoughts. If you are able to make a choice that you will have freedom and stay true to that, you have already set yourself apart from everyone else. You are on your way to obtaining all your heart's desires.

Transformation Must Happen

One of the biggest blessings I have received from being able to be free is the person I have had to become and the person I am becoming in order to help others. "Freedom isn't free." It requires you to become a different person in order to obtain freedom. As a coach, this is one of the most rewarding things to see in a person-- to see a person transform from who they were to who they become on their journey to freedom. I love to see people change their thoughts by hearing their words. I love to see someone who thought they were shy become the most outgoing person in the room. For true freedom to happen in your life, you must be ready to change into that person. Think about this: if you were already the person you needed to be, you would already be free.

Creativity Takes Courage

One of the most courageous things to do is go against the grain. I was taught that in order to live the best life, I must be willing to go to school, get good grades, get a good job, and I would live happily ever after. However, like most of you reading this book, that wasn't necessarily the case. In fact, most people today don't even work in their field of study. Today, more than ever, college graduates are unable to even find a job. They are where I was and going from temp job to temp job. I can remember when I made a

18

decision to go after freedom and leave my job. The first thing the majority of the people in my life said was that I was crazy. It was definitely a world of the unknown but in order to go after it, I was required to be a bit creative. I'm also not telling you to quit your job; however, I do want you to know that a choice will eventually be made on someone controlling your time versus you controlling it. When I say creativity is important, I mean thinking outside the box. I'm thankful that when I made this decision, I was positioned to meet the right people to help me in my journey. A mentor entered my life which changed my life forever. I believe that is why you bought this book. I know that once you are done you will most definitely have an idea that will allow your creative juices to flow. It's time to think outside the box!

Now, do I believe you can be free with *just* not having a job? No, I don't. However, this is based on my definition of freedom. I couldn't be on a timed schedule. For you, freedom may be different. This book is not designed to create your definition of freedom, but to make you aware of what's available to you.

Faith is The Ultimate State

Faith, in my opinion, is one of the most powerful words in the English dictionary. Faith means you love, and love is a universal feeling, which is felt by every living being on this earth. Do not be surprised when I say 'living beings', because it is not just an attribute of human beings. Plants and animals are also acquainted with this strange emotion. In order for you to take that first step, you must have faith in yourself. You must love yourself. You must have faith in your idea of freedom. You must fall in love with your idea of freedom.

Challenges Will Come

One of the keys to obtaining any goal in life is to also know what challenges you will face. I believe that if you already know what is ahead of you in your journey, then you will be able to better handle it.

When you know the challenges will come - because they will - you can't lose! You'll never quit! In this book, I will show you how to handle those challenges.

Now keep in mind, I don't believe that you will be able to predict ALL challenges. However, know that there will be challenges. I love the quote "It's not what happens to you but how you handle what happens to you that will impact your life" Author Unknown.

It's Possible, Not Guaranteed

The reason people keep doing certain things is because of their belief in the possibility. I am a true believer that all things are possible to those who believe. One of the things that has helped me believe in the possibility is my circle of influence, my environment, and my words. I look forward to raising your belief in the possibility. In most cases, the reason people don't believe in freedom is just because they haven't been made aware. You will now be made aware of the possibilities. I'm so excited for you!

Educate Yourself

Education is a never-ending process. I love to learn about how to apply new techniques and skills to my life. Some say education is the process of gaining information about the surrounding world, while knowledge is something very different. They are right. But then again, information cannot be converted into knowledge without education. Education makes us capable of interpreting things, among other things. Never stop strengthening your knowledge in health, spirituality, relationships, and business. Education is required for growth.

Live Your Life

Your life is yours alone, so don't let anyone keep you from living it. I believe that we must always remember that we are only given one of these lives here as the person we are today, and it's important to go for yours. For too long I was living a life of being complacent until I had a paradigm shift that took place in my life. It was when my father passed away from lung cancer. It confirmed that life is just too short here and to not live it to the fullest and go after your dreams is just selling yourself short. Live your life to the fullest and never let anyone steal your dreams. This is true freedom to me. To be able to live your life how you want to live it. Again, I am so excited for you because it's now time for you to live your life!

Have Peace

What do I mean when I speak of peace? I mean being in a state of mind where you are content. When you know what you know and that it's already done for you, it allows for you to stay in a place of calmness. It means not being emotional. It means not letting anything or anyone break your focus on where you are going. I remember the months that I have had the most success in life were also the months that I was emotionally sound. It's important to follow the instructions in this book and when you do, it'll allow you to stay in a state of peace.

<u>Chapter 2: Take Responsibility</u>

"If you take responsibility for yourself you will develop a hunger to accomplish your dreams."

Les Brown

Change Begins with You

The most important thing to remember about change is that in order for change to happen in your life, you must change first. It's interesting to me that even within the industry that changed my life, I didn't see success happen until I started to work on myself. It would intrigue me how so many people would always look for the results to happen right away, but the person they were hadn't even changed a bit. You must understand that everything in your life is a direct result of who you have been. The life you live today is based on the choices you made in the past. Your life is based on your thoughts. Now, I know that for most people, they don't want to hear that. However, think about it. Your job is your job because you thought of it. Your outfit you have on today is because you thought of it. You are reading this book because you thought of it. So, if you want your life to change, you must change what you are thinking of. It always starts with you. It's not an overnight process either, but if you can contribute every day to becoming that person, then change is surely on its way.

Practice Forgiveness

I have coached several people and families that have had the difficulty of forgiving. I have even had it in my life. If you don't learn to forgive, then you will never be able to move on. I see it all the time. People will blame their circumstance because of what someone did in their past. However, remember that we can determine our future by what we choose to focus on. Learning to forgive will empower you and has even been known to help strengthen your health. This isn't easy, but for true freedom to be obtained, you can't hold on to the past.

This means you need to forgive anyone who did bad things to you in the past and even in the present, as well as in the future. This is especially true if you have had a grudge against someone for a long time. The way you know you've forgiven them is by asking yourself if you can either wish them well or be grateful for them. If you can truthfully answer "yes," you have indeed forgiven them. Forgiveness is so vital to our dreams in life that if we don't do it and hold any resentment, fear, or any frustration inside, it can literally block us from getting what we want in life. Lastly, we must learn to forgive ourselves for what we do to others and ourselves. If we can look at ourselves in the mirror and say we love ourselves, we are on our way to experiencing the life we want.

I personally want to help you with some things that I've done in my past to help me with forgiveness. Now keep in mind, there's no single manual for forgiveness, but I believe this will be a good step in the right direction.

Here are four steps to forgiveness that I use:

1.   **Express the emotion.** Let yourself feel hurt and angry. Speak aloud how you feel and if you can, express how you feel to the person. If you are not able to talk directly to that person, you can use a stand-in friend or even an empty chair. Write a letter and instead of giving it to them, burn it or simply tear it up. Shout your emotions at the top of your lungs while you're in the car, alone, with the windows down. LET IT OUT FULLY.

2.   **Understand why.** If you are able to, find out why this person did it. You may not agree with it, but it is good to get the understanding. If you can't speak with that person personally, you can even write it down as if you were that person. When I look back at a lot of people in my life who have done me wrong, I just wrote in a letter as if I were them. It's always allowed me to really understand their point of view. It allows me to forgive.

3.   **Rebuild safety.** Before you forgive, make sure this won't happen again. That might mean an apology, reassurance from the person in question, distance or stronger boundaries. Sometimes this may even mean that there will be a season of separation. Thinking of this reminds me of one of my favorite poems.

Reason, Season, or Lifetime

People come into your life for a reason, a season or a lifetime. When you figure out which one it is, you will know what to do for each person.

When someone is in your life for a REASON, it is usually to meet a need you have expressed. They have come to assist you through a difficulty; to provide you with guidance and support; to aid you physically, emotionally or spiritually. They may seem like a godsend, and they are. They are there for the reason you need them to be.

Then, without any wrongdoing on your part or at an inconvenient time, this person will say or do something to bring the relationship to an end. Sometimes they die. Sometimes they walk away.

Sometimes they act up and force you to take a stand. What we must realize is that our need has been met, our desire fulfilled; their work is done. The prayer you sent up has been answered and now
it is time to move on.

Some people come into your life for a SEASON, because your turn has come to share, grow or learn. They bring you an experience of peace or make you laugh. They may teach you something you have never done. They usually give you an unbelievable amount of joy. Believe it. It is real. But only for a season.

LIFETIME relationships teach you lifetime lessons; things you must build upon in order to have a solid emotional foundation. Your job is to accept the lesson, love the person, and put what you have learned to use in all other relationships and areas of your life. It is said that love is blind, but friendship is

27

clairvoyant.

— Unknown

4.   **Let go.** Perhaps it's the hardest part; making a conscious decision not to hold a grudge. If you're in a relationship, this means not bringing up past transgressions. By letting go, you give up your role as the victim and become equals again. It's a promise to yourself to stop ruminating and to fully move on.

Be Grateful

I am so happy and grateful now that you are reading this book! Don't we have so much to be grateful for? Think about it. There was a time that reading a book like this, written by a woman like me, was forbidden. To even have the means to read this book is amazing. There are some people in this world who can't even read. There was someone today who didn't even wake up. WOW... The attitude of gratitude is so important. You can never have more if you aren't grateful for what you have now. One of the things that I use to help me with my gratitude is the affirmation you read at the beginning of this section. "I am so happy and grateful now that..." I actually got this from the movie "The Secret" by Rhonda Byrne.

People who lack gratitude always seem to find themselves living in poverty or not having the lifestyle they wish to have. They look upon themselves as lower than anything else and wonder why they can't be better than what they are. The primary reason for this is that they lack acceptance to what they want and do not show to the universe what they want or deserve to have.

There is no doubt that you get what you ask for, and you get it in abundance when you put a lot of effort into it. By showing gratitude, you are showing that the effort you put forth was in tune with what you desired; and you will obtain more of what you wish.

This is why when you look at rich people, you notice they get richer. They have a debt of gratitude and show it every day. This way, they are telling the universe that they are glad they have all these riches and deserve them. The universe responds by giving them more.

If a person does have abundance but does not show gratitude, they will eventually lose it. This is because they are telling the universe that they do not deserve it. When the universe perceives this, the universe stops delivering.

On the other hand, if a person lacks abundance, but shows gratitude for what they have, the universe will see that and will in turn give the person more of what that person wishes. This way, that person does not lack for very long.

If a person lacks abundance and does not show gratitude, they will continue to live with lack because they have not shown they deserve more.

Also keep in mind that being grateful is not just about what you have, but also being grateful for what you will have. That means you are grateful for something that is coming in your future and because you have expressed the gratitude for what is already yours, the universe has no other option but to start moving in and changing so that what you are focusing on, you'll have. It's a principle that what you think about you will have. The law of attraction is all about your gratitude.

The reason most people never get to advance in life is because they only focus on what's not happening in their life, instead of focusing on what they want. They play the victim role instead of the victor role. You may not realize this, but gratitude is very powerful. Having gratitude connects you to the Universe or God, depending on how you look at it.

Without gratitude, you have no power, since the two connect together. And by using our minds for positive things, we are in reality using the power we have to produce the reality we want. So, when we show gratitude, we are in fact producing high energy positive vibrations of thought. This high energy can only lead to one manifestation – great achievements.

As you can see, I have spent a lot of time talking about gratitude as it is most definitely one important factor if you truly desire to have a life of freedom. Honestly, out of all the subjects in this book, the topic of gratitude is probably one of the most powerful which will allow you to be able to do all these different things within this book.

Let Go and Trust

It's hard to just say let go and trust, but that's something that you used to do as a baby. Think about when you first learned how to walk. That's pretty scary if you think about it, because so much can happen, but as a baby you weren't taught how to doubt. You just saw what other people were doing and you trusted you could do it. You must make sure to stay focused on where you are going. If you are a believer, then you must also believe that if it can happen for one, it can happen for all. You must be willing to let go of all your old thoughts and beliefs that counteract with your future. You must be willing to let go of people who don't believe in your belief as well. Trust that if they love you, then they will understand and you will inspire them and they will one day believe as well. You must let go of your fears and know that you will be protected. Let go of doubt, because doubt will keep you from ever getting to true freedom. It will keep you chained up forever. Let go and trust in the future, because the past is the past.

Words are Powerful

I am a believer that the world was created with words, so if I believe that, then I also believe that all words create life. Of course we know that thoughts are powerful, but also remember that when you actually speak your thoughts, you've just increased you power

31

by multitudes. You must learn to be very conscious of the words you speak. Not only being grateful but speaking the right words are very important. Also, don't allow others to speak opposite of what you want to happen to you. If there is something that I am believing for, I never let someone speak opposite of that belief around me, not even myself. This is also why I don't watch the news because hearing all the Constant Negative News only allows me to believe that there is no good in the world. But that's not the truth! Trust me, there are many more great things happening than the bad things. Ninety-seven percent of the population likes to hear the drama. Three percent, which also makes up the top income earners in the world, focus on the positive. Words, words, words are so, so, so powerful. One book I would recommend that you read, which my mentor told me about, is "Hung by the Tongue" by Francis Martin.

Start Small

When I say start small, it's not the same as thinking small. There is a big difference. It's ok to think big. In fact, I recommend that the bigger the vision, the better. However, don't try to build Rome in a day. You want to set a game-plan and start working at your journey to freedom day by day. Start with setting goals. In fact, I am going to show you how to set goals and make it so specific that you'll be able to teach others how to do the same. However, the reason I mention goal setting is because a lot of the time when I ask people their goals, they start off wanting to do way too much. Then, when they are not able to accomplish their goal, they are ready to give up so easily. The key to this is setting steps to reach to your ultimate goal which, of course, is Freedom. At least I believe that is why you bought this book. Think about it. It took you however old you are today to become who you are today, so we know that for our lives to change, we can't expect for it to happen overnight. In Chapter 4, I give step-by-step instructions on how to set goals. Trust me. This will blow your mind. I have found that 97% of people don't know that goal setting is more than just saying what you want. There is a process to it. I look forward to showing you how and also seeing your goals.

Put Up Visual Signs

I talk more about this later in the book, but I wanted to make sure to briefly let you know that what you see is also just as important as what you think about. We actually think in pictures. Purple Elephant! Okay, so I know you are asking yourself why I just wrote "Purple Elephant!" Well, when you read it, what did you think of? You guessed it: a purple elephant. So I am right; we think in pictures. It's also safe to say that your thoughts can be controlled by what you see. This is why I know that it doesn't just stop with thinking and speaking what you want, but you must also see what you want. In fact, I have a treat for you when I discuss visualizing your future in Chapter 4. Don't skip to this chapter, but I promise you are going to love the goodies!

Look at Positive vs. Negative

By now this should make total sense to you as we have talked about this before, but to make sure you understand, I want to keep it fresh in your mind. Now, negative experiences are somewhat impossible to avoid. That's life. There will always be good and bad moments. It's not what happens to you that determines the outcome; it's how you handle it. When you learn to focus your attention on the good versus the bad, you will see that the good will always prevail.

Let me give you an example of how what you focus on always comes to fruition. The first time you do a task, such as driving a car to a new location, you have to focus and fully concentrate on remembering which turns to take and what landmarks to look out for. After you have taken that route several times, however, you are able to do it with minimal conscious effort. You can let your mind wander to other thoughts while you make those lefts and rights and pass the landmarks, because the repetition imprints the route on the circuitry of your brain. The same effect is found when positive information is used to counter negativity. This is why positive affirmations and repeated positive thought works. Hello! The brain learned the new road and drives the route on its own through repetition. So the brain re-learns a new positive thinking route too!

So don't give up! Identify the negative, take control, and do things to reverse it. You have to learn to train your brain. And as with everything else we learn how to do in life, it starts to become second nature and easier. It's really an easy thing to do. We tend to make it harder than it is! So, get started. Keep thinking positively and do more, more, more positive. Submerge yourself into it. Swim in it if you can. Surround yourself with as much as you can. Speak it as much as you can, read it, watch it, hear it, do it.

Empower Yourself

So many times, individuals I coach are looking for me to help them to be empowered, but the truth is the person who really keeps you empowered is you. Self-motivation is the best motivation of all. When you are only empowered by other people, it means that you depend on other people to make you happy. The key to true freedom is to find a way to stay empowered yourself. Of course, I do recommend having special people in your life that you look up to and who inspire you. However, the key is that once you have found individuals who have given you that initial empowerment, you are able to find a way to stay empowered. That's true character. Being able to stay excited long after the person has left or the event is over. Yours words, your images, and your emotions are most definitely what will help you to stay empowered. I will, of course, cover this in later chapters in more depth.

Step Outside Your Comfort Zone

There's no room for adventure and excitement in your comfort zone; in fact, over time you might feel overwhelmed and trapped by boredom and fear. Perhaps it's time to stretch those limits a little. Not only will your life become more exciting, but you'll also build confidence.

I once had someone ask me how I got over being shy, and the truth is that, honestly, I've never gotten over the fear of talking to people. But I did make a decision that I wouldn't allow the fact that I thought I was shy keep me from stepping outside my comfort zone. The reason I say that I thought I was shy is because honestly, the reason you are the way you are is because someone put that belief into you; you were told that was who you were, and you believed it. Our actions come from our beliefs, so in order to change our beliefs, we must act. My advice in getting over a fear of something is actually going after it. Take gradual steps towards it. For example, if you are shy like I was, start off with just smiling at five people today. Tomorrow say hello. The next day, say hello, and then introduce yourself. The next day, say hello, introduce yourself, and give a compliment. Start doing small things towards your fears and watch. Eventually that fear will no longer control your life.

Never Give Up

I wanted to share an amazing story with you, which I actually have posted in my office. This is one of my favorite stories, period, and has allowed me to stay focused. Before you read it, I want to let you know that you are absolutely amazing and that everything you've been through in life has a reason, and you will soon find how your story will only help so many other people if you just believe. You can never give up on your choice to obtain freedom. I'm looking forward to the breakthrough you will receive from this book! Congratulations in advance, but this is just the beginning! Enjoy!

There was a couple who took a trip to England to shop in a beautiful antique store to celebrate their 25th wedding anniversary. They both liked antiques and pottery, and especially teacups. Spotting an exceptional cup, they asked, 'May we see that? We've never seen a cup quite so beautiful.'

As the lady handed it to them, suddenly the teacup spoke, "You don't understand. I have not always been a teacup. There was a time when I was just a lump of red clay. My master took me and rolled me, pounded and patted me over and over and I yelled out, 'Don't do that. I don't like it! Let me alone.' But he only smiled, and gently said, 'Not yet!' "Then WHAM! I was placed on a spinning wheel and suddenly I was spun around and around and around. 'Stop it! I'm getting so dizzy! I'm going to be sick,' I screamed. But the master only nodded and said, quietly, 'Not yet.'

He spun me and poked and prodded and bent me out of shape to suit himself and then... Then he put me in the oven. I never felt such heat. I yelled and knocked and pounded at the door. Help! Get me

37

out of here! I could see him through the opening and I could read his lips as he shook his head from side to side, 'Not yet.'

When I thought I couldn't bear it another minute, the door opened. He carefully took me out and put me on the shelf, and I began to cool. Oh, that felt so good! Ah, this is much better, I thought. But after I cooled he picked me up and he brushed and painted me all over. The fumes were horrible. I thought I would gag. 'Oh, please, stop it, stop it!' I cried. He only shook his head and said. 'Not yet!'

Then suddenly he put me back into the oven. Only it was not like the first one. This was twice as hot and I just knew I would suffocate. I begged. I pleaded. I screamed. I cried. I was convinced I would never make it. I was ready to give up. Just then the door opened and he took me out and again placed me on the shelf, where I cooled and waited ——- and waited, wondering, 'What's he going to do to me next?' An hour later he handed me a mirror and said 'Look at yourself.' And I did. I said, 'That's not me, that couldn't be me. It's beautiful. I'm beautiful!'

Quietly he spoke: 'I want you to remember,' then he said, 'I know it hurt to be rolled and pounded and patted, but had I just left you alone, you'd have dried up. I know it made you dizzy to spin around on the wheel, but if I had stopped, you would have crumbled. I know it hurt and it was hot and disagreeable in the oven, but if I hadn't put you there, you would have cracked. I know the fumes were bad when I brushed and painted you all over, but if I hadn't done that, you never would have hardened. You would not have had any color in your life. If I hadn't put you back in that second oven, you wouldn't have survived for long because the hardness would not have held. Now you are a finished product. Now you are what I had in mind when I first began with you.'

38

The moral of this story is this: God knows what He's doing for each of us. He is the potter, and we are His clay. He will mold us and make us, and expose us to just enough pressures of just the right kinds that we may be made into a flawless piece of work to fulfill His good, pleasing and perfect will.

So when life seems hard, and you are being pounded and patted and pushed almost beyond endurance; when your world seems to be spinning out of control; when you feel like you are in a fiery furnace of trials; when life seems to 'stink,' try this....

Brew a cup of your favorite tea in your prettiest teacup, sit down and think on this story and then, have a little talk with the Potter."

– Author Unknown

Chapter 3: Visualize your Future

"Vision is the art of being able to see what others can't see with their physical eye."

Taurea V. Avant

Know What You Want

Before you can even start visualizing anything, you need to know exactly what it is that you want. For me I can remember times where I was visualizing things that other people want it for me. The unfortunate thing about that is it wasn't things that moves me. So I found myself being in many states of inactivity. It wasn't until I decided that I would start visualizing the things that I wanted. And so in order to do that I had to know exactly what it was that I wanted. Yes, I wanted to have more money but what did I want to do with that money. A lot of times people will visualize money but not never assigning it to anything. That's a scary place to be. I can tell you almost 100% of the time if you set a goal to just only make money but you don't assign what it will buy you will always spend it on things you have no idea what you spent it on. So now you have to start July's and what it is that you want. Do you want to take a trip? Do you want to buy a new car? Do you want to get a new house? Do you want to pay off some debt? You want to buy new clothes? it really doesn't matter what it is that you want but you must be specific as to what it is that you want.

Be Specific

So I know I've already said be specific. But I want to break it down even more. A lot of times out here people say I want to be able to buy a new house. Well that's a great visualization to start off with. You also need to be specific as to what the house will look like.

42

How many rooms do you want? How many bathrooms? What do you want the interior to look like? Do you want two floors? How many cars do you want to fit in your garage? Do you want to guess house? Now I understand you might be saying to yourself This is just way too much. I promise you it's absolutely is not. If it's not a house that you want but you want to take a trip, you need to know exactly what it's going to. How much are the flights? How much is the room? How much will you need for food? Where is it that you want to go? When you figure out all of these things you can even go and get pictures of the hotel of the airline all of that. And post it up. The more specific you are, the more you believe and what it is that you're looking to achieve.

Take Daily Actions

Now that you know what it is that you want, you have to take daily actions towards getting it done. For example, I had to go to increase my database. If I increase my database, that means that I would increase my customers. If I increase my customers, then that means I would increase my income. If I increase my income, that means I would be able to take the trip that I wanted to take for my birthday to London. Okay so let's go back to how it was going to get to London. It all started with me getting more subscribers. So I know an order for me to get to London. I hope this is making sense. So now on a daily basis my email list that I can then be able to convert to the next step. You see, success is not about doing some Grand action one time. In fact, I tell people all the time. Success can be quite boring. Because success is seriously over a long period of time. The person who can stay going the longest and stay excited about these small tasks is the person that will always win!

Don't Focus on What's NOT Happening

So this is going to be difficult. Most people like to focus on what is not happening versus what is happening. A lot of times what you may think is not working is actually working it's just taking time to build up. The truth is that it can take at least 90 days to even see a harvest of a small sort from the work that you are doing. So, don't focus on the things that are not happening. Focus on the things that are. For example, instead of focusing on the money. I would probably focus on the fact that I am getting more subscribers. I would focus on how many subscribers I'm getting on a daily basis. This is a great thing. Now if I'm not getting any subscribers then of course in, will not go up. So, the key is that you must focus on the things that are working. Also, I most definitely do not like the focus on the negative. When you focus on the negative it will cause you to have negative energy. So I do my best to focus on the things that are working. I speak with my coach. And I take new actions. Whatever it is that you focus on will always be your truth. So focus on what you want and not the opposite.

See Yourself Already There

A lot of times people will ask me how does it feel to be able to achieve certain goals? The truth is that once I have hit my goal, I've already experienced it long before it happened. For me it's the process of getting to the goal that is honestly the most exciting. That is where I'm visualizing myself already there. I already see myself with that new car. I already see myself with that new house. I already see myself with this many clients or customers or students. I already see myself with this many books. I already see myself standing on the stage speaking to stay at Stadium. I already see myself best friends with Oprah. You see the truth is this. If you don't already see yourself there, it's very hard to get there. If by chance you are but you never saw yourself there you will probably lose it! You must do this. And the way that you program your subconscious. The person that does this the most, with the proper action steps and the proper coaching in the fastest!

<u>Chapter 4: Control Your Finances</u>

"Ninety-eight percent of the population will end up dead or broke by age 65. Only two percent of the population will succeed."

Dani Johnson

Set Financial Goals

How much money do you want to make 90 days from now? How about five years from now? More often than not, the reason why we never make more than we do today is because we don't set financial goals. If you don't set it, you'll never achieve it. The first step in controlling your finances is knowing how much money you NEED to make and how much money you WANT to make. The difference between the two is the money you "need to make" is what you use to pay your bills. The money that you "want to make" will be the disposable income that you have to truly be able to be free and live the life of your dreams. In this chapter, I will show you some techniques of what to do with your money once you've made it. I know most people think they need to know how to make the money first. That is where I have to disagree, because until you know what to do with your money so that it increases, the HOW TO doesn't matter. I know this personally because I've made a lot of money and lost a lot of that money. This is because no one ever taught me the right money principles of what to do with a dollar. I have to give many thanks to my mentors over the years that have helped me tremendously with this.

Track What You Spend

The first step to controlling your finances is tracking what you spend. I started carrying a small notepad with me every day and writing down every expense I made that day, even if it was $.50. I did this because I am an impulsive spender, and it would come to the end of the month and I wouldn't understand what I had spent my money on. Even if you aren't an impulsive spender, having this notepad will help you. Because I knew that I had to pull this book out every time I bought something, I would skip buying items just because I didn't feel like pulling out the notepad. Also, at the end of the day, I would total up all my expenses and separate what was important and what was not. This also helped me a lot to track my spending habits. I found that certain times of the month I would buy certain things. I love to shop, so there would be certain days that I would get that itch. Try this for at least 90 days and watch how you become very conscious of your spending. In fact, I have a little gift for you to help you with tracking your spending. Download your copy of my tracking document by going to: Bonus.Asixfigurevision.com

Open Separate Accounts

Now that you are tracking your spending, you will also want to make sure you are tracking your savings and income. I was so excited when my mentor taught me what to do with a dollar. What was even more incredible is that in all my years of college, I never had this type of training. I only was ever shown how to spend money; never how to keep it. I've always lived paycheck to paycheck, and that's probably because my parents lived that way, and their parents did too. Think about it - what are the spending habits of your parents? I'm pretty sure whatever it is they do or did, you probably do the same. Well, today we are going to change that. I'm going to show you how to make your money work for you! First, you will need to have at least 4 different accounts. You can have them with separate banks, or all the same. I have some in different banks and I'll tell you why. In fact, I want you to make this commitment that you will at least open two different accounts by the time you have finished reading this chapter.

Give Back Account

First, you must always remember that it's so important to sow a seed to get a harvest. I have a goal to tithe or donate 10% of my income to my church or charity of choice. I used to have a challenge with this when I had all my accounts attached, so to make it easier for myself, I opened what I call my 'charity account'. This should be the first account you put money into. Remember, you can never receive if you aren't willing to give. Every time I have been consistent with my giving, my harvest has always produced massive fruit. This is a law. Always remember that the ability to obtain wealth was not all your doing. It was given to you by God or your higher power. Whatever you choose to believe in, I believe that if it weren't for Him, I wouldn't have these blessings I have today. To give is to receive. The Law of Reciprocity states in the spiritual world that when you give, it will be given to you for every action. In the physical world, it states that there is an equal and opposite reaction. Smile at another person, and he'll probably smile back at you. Be critical of others, and they'll respond in kind. As you give, you will receive. Give generously, and you'll receive in like measure.

Savings Account

The next account is your savings, which you do not touch by any means necessary. This should comprise 10% of your income. What I love most about my savings account is that I can see it grow. When you see your accounts grow, it motivates you to keep going. I remember times when my account was negative. Man oh man, was that a dream stealer; however, seeing my account today with multiple commas only motivates me that what I'm doing is working. By no means do you want to touch this account. NEVER touch it! I don't care if all of your other accounts are at zero, never touch this account. To make it more difficult to withdraw from my savings account, I keep it at a separate bank than all my other accounts.

I even opened a credit union account where the credit union isn't located in my state, so I would physically have to go to a service center to make transactions. Also, I don't have an ATM card for this account. Because I have made it so hard to withdraw from, it has helped me tremendously in not touching it. The only time I really get to see how it's growing is when they mail me the statement. I even don't know the login information, so I can view it online! Make it tough and you won't even want to bother.

Bills/Taxes Account

Your bills/taxes account should have the highest monthly deposit. Thirty percent of your income is what you should put toward your bills, and another 30% will go towards your taxes. I have a checking and savings within the same bank for these accounts. I put 30% in my checking and 30% in my savings. The reason I put so much in the savings is because I'm self-employed, so that means I am responsible for paying my own taxes. Word from the wise is that you never ever want to play with the IRS. So get that out of the way now! I know from personal experience that the IRS does not play with their money. I don't care if you only owe them a few hundred dollars - they can make your life a living nightmare!

Keep in mind, if you are finding that 30% of your income is not enough to pay the bills, then attempt to find ways to cut back on your monthly expenses. Some things you might consider doing includes cutting the cable off, reducing your cellular bill, or cutting back on the electricity you use. There are many ways to do it, but make sure to figure something out. This can be tough, but it is necessary. Many people that I've coached have even had to move out of their homes to help on expenses. Keep this in mind - it's only temporary! This is how most people find themselves in trouble - because their monthly expenses are way out of their budget. When they finally make a decision to cut back, they are already in way over their heads, and it's too late. Don't let this be you!

Now, if you also have your taxes taken out of your check, then your monthly expenses checking account can be 30% to 40% of your income because you don't have to necessarily worry about your taxes. Put the other 20% in your tax savings account, because if you earn more than a certain amount, you will be responsible for paying additional taxes.

Investments Account

There are many ways to invest: special accounts, bonds, as well as stocks and mutual funds. I would recommend hiring someone who can help you with this or going to your bank to identify what would be best for you, based upon how much you have to invest and what type of return you are looking for. Another type of investment is investing in *yourself.* Personal

53

development has always been the best investment. I believe that personal development is something you never stop doing. I have more books and audios in my home than any other type of collection, and trust me, I own a lot of shoes! I've invested in seminars, books, and audios. I've also noticed that my investment into personal development has increased in money as my income has increased.

"Do Whatever" Account

The most important account of them all is your "Do Whatever" account. Why? Because this is the account where you keep the money to buy the items that motivate you. The clothes, shoes, cars – whatever it is that you want. This is the account where you purchase those items that aren't required for you to live, but rather, they are the items that you live *for*. A dream trip to Fiji, a Chanel watch, a Hermes bag. These are some of the items that I will purchase with my "Do Whatever" account. Now, I know what you are saying. "Taurea, I don't need these types of things." That's no problem! These are just some of the things that I love. What are some of the things you would love to have if money was not an issue? If you could go anywhere in the world, where would you go? Well, this is the account you would use towards the items on your dream board. Keep in mind though, you may save to it or you can spend from it every day, but only put 10% of your income into this account. If you don't have the money available in this account to buy those shoes, then keep saving until you have it available. This is what I also like to call the W.I.F.F.M. (What's In It For Me) account. When you close your eyes and envision what motivates you, even if it's a Ferrari or a mission trip to Africa, then that's what this account will help you to accomplish.

Multiple Streams of Income

Have you ever heard the quote, "Never put all your eggs into one basket?" What this means is that if your only means of income is coming from just one source, then you most definitely want to start looking at additional ways to earn income. Now, I don't mean go and get another job. I believe that two jobs are for two people. I also don't mean to go out and do two types of the same industry. I remember a young lady I was coaching decided that she would get into direct sales. If you know my story, you know I am an advocate for the direct sales industry; however, I am not an advocate of trying to work for multiple companies at one time. She thought it would be great to join two different companies, and even though they were both great companies with great products, she ended up becoming frustrated because she would always find herself trying to figure what to sell to her customers. A confused mind does nothing.

In the next chapter, I talk about why you should have multiple streams of income. I also give you a few ideas of what I have done, as well as what some of my students have achieved.

Tax Write Offs

Another way to be in control of your finances is to not give so much of it away to the government. Every year around January, so many people are so excited because they know they are going to get what we here in America call their "tax refund check." However, what always ruffled my feathers was the word "refund." That word lets you know that this is just your money being given back to you. So with that said, I decided very early that I would find ways to keep my money upfront. When I found out there were so many ways to save on taxes, I was dumbfounded because I couldn't believe that for all these years, I had been completely ignorant to them! I'm thankful I had the right person introduced into my life that helped me to better understand my taxes.

One way to find out about tax benefits is to speak to a tax specialist at the beginning of the year about the different ways you can save on taxes. Now keep in mind, I am not a tax specialist, so be sure to confirm this with someone who is licensed in this field; however, I would like to show you some of the things I've done to help me with my taxes.

- **Donate to Charity or Gifting** –Donating cash, property, clothing, household items or other goods is a great way to get a tax break and help a worthy cause at the same time. If you donate cash to an eligible charity this year, you can generally deduct the amount you contribute when you pay your taxes. You can also donate property and stocks. Another way is to gift money or property to people. Be sure to always keep receipts of all transactions, as they are required.

- **Accelerate Deductible Expenses** - Do you have medical bills, state and local taxes, mortgage payments, or property taxes to pay? If so, you may want to consider making those payments before the year ends. Even if they aren't due until next year, any payments you make before December 31st are deductible on this year's tax return.

- **Pay Bills Earlier** - Making an extra mortgage payment or paying off outstanding dental or medical bills is a great way to offset your tax bill. Just make sure you aren't subject to the Alternative Minimum Tax (which generally applies to high-income or upper-middle income households) and that you plan to itemize your deductions.

- **Self-Employment** – I know I've already talked about having a home-based business, but remember when I said it was one of the best investments I've ever made? The reason is not just because of the great income I've received from the industry but also because of the tax benefits. By having a home-based business, the government actually gives me over 400 different tax benefits. A lot of items, including those that were bills, are now considered write-offs. I love this aspect of the industry because there are people who have been able to start a home-based business, and even though they didn't really need that additional income, they were able to save hundreds to even thousands in taxes simply because they had a home-based business. It just makes good business sense.

• **Offset Your Capital Gains** – When the end of the year comes, take a good look at your investment portfolio and consider selling losing stocks to offset your capital gains. The loss from the stocks will counter the gains acquired from others, lowering your tax bill and softening the blow from under-performing stocks.

• **Contribute the Maximum to Retirement Accounts** - Retirement accounts are an excellent way to lower your tax bill, so make sure you're getting the most out of this break. If you can swing it financially, raising your 401k contributions to the maximum amount allowed will really take a bite out of your tax liability. You might also consider contributing year-end bonuses to a tax-deferred 401k account.

• **Flexible Spending Accounts** - Does your employer or bank offer a flexible spending account? It's a great way to save cash by using tax-free money to pay eligible medical and child care expenses. You can also use it to pay for medical or dental expenses that aren't covered (or not fully covered) by insurance, like glasses and certain over-the-counter medications. You can even set up an account to pay for child care while you work or attend school.

Money Isn't Bad

I had to include this topic because as a young child, I had a lot of friends who believed that rich people were bad people. I remember even being told by my parents many things about money that could also have affected my belief in money. I wasn't brought up around the rich and wealthy; however, I've always had a desire to be rich and wealthy. I've always had a special respect for money. I've heard so many people say that money is the root of all evil; however, that is wrong. It is "the love of money," to be exact, that the scripture states is wrong. "For the love of money is the root of all evil: which while some coveted after, they have erred from the faith, and pierced themselves through with many sorrows." So many people get confused about money, and in turn, they end up fearing it. I've never believed that money is bad, but you will be surprised that there are a lot of people who believe it is. However, if you think about it, if we don't have money, then how would we live? Now, if you have a bad spirit, money will only enhance that aspect of your spirit. However, you are reading this book, so I don't believe that would be true. To have money only allows you to do more of what you want to do. Money is going to be required to truly be able to have freedom.

Surround Yourself with Others Who Have Money

One thing I've learned to do is make sure that I put myself in the right environments; environments of wealth. In fact, I wrote this book in some of the most expensive hotels and meeting areas in the country. When I think of freedom, I also envision those in wealthy environments. If you want to increase your finances, be around people who are earning the type of income you desire to earn. I've also found that these types of people are also the ones who are more willing to be of help. I love to be around people who like helping other people. So, go out and find the most expensive restaurants and hotels, and hang out there - even if it's only to drink a cup of coffee and people-watch. Soon you'll find yourself talking to them. The next thing you know, you're at a private event as their guest. If you keep on, you'll soon find yourself hosting an event and inviting *them*. Be around the right people and watch how your income will grow. True freedom also means not having to worry about things like your finances, so be sure to be around people who don't have those worries.

Chapter 5: Develop Multiple Streams

"You are your wealth. The money that flows to you is just a by-product of your non-financial resources."

Robert G Allen

Develop Multiple Streams

Money tends to be the number one topic of discussion when I start talking about freedom. I have heard some people tell me that money isn't everything; however, it kind of ranks up there along with oxygen. Here in this world, you pretty much need it for everything. I have always been a true believer that the best way to make money is through multiple streams, and in this chapter, I will explain to you why you should have multiple streams of income as well as give you a few ideas of how to obtain them. The great thing about this chapter is that you have already learned the right money principles of what to do with a dollar. Now that you know what to do with a dollar, it is my goal to help you obtain some. Also remember the true purpose of having multiple streams of income is so that you are able to truly live out your passions and experience true freedom.

Another great thing about this chapter is that it really will open your eyes to what having money can do. This is the chapter that will help you realize exactly how important money really is.

In this section of the chapter, I will show you some examples of why you should have multiple streams of income.

Rising Health Care Costs

I remember that I used to think that in order to have my health covered, I would need a job. However, even if you do have a job, you are still at risk of not having the right coverage for your health needs. What are you doing for those additional expenses that could come up with your health care? Because of having multiple streams of income, I actually have a separate healthcare savings account that has helped me tremendously. And simply having a job might not be enough; the fact is, there are so many of us working full-time without any healthcare benefits at all. I actually went to college and got my bachelor's degree, then went years without any healthcare coverage because my job didn't provide it and I couldn't afford it—which is the reason why I decided to take my income into my own hands.

There is No Job Security

When you put the words job and security together, what does that feel like? To me I can't help but to laugh. YEAH RIGHT! There is no such thing as job security. Forget about the days when you could work one job for 20 to 30 years. Nothing is secure anymore. You have jobs beings outsourced for pennies on the dollar. We are even to the point where technology taking over some our jobs! Because of the lack of jobs, we also have people willing to take jobs for less pay than what they were used to. Unfortunately, even with all this happening, the cost of living is still going up. I don't know about you, but this doesn't sound like freedom to me.

Paying for College

I think to be able to pay for college up front without the use of federal aid is a blessing. I have helped so many students make additional income to the point where the money they were making was more than what I made with a college degree. However, I think that if you can make enough money to help with expenses, that's also a blessing. Why not start now? Why not start building a college fund to prepare you for the future?

Take Control of Your Income

The one thing I never enjoyed was allowing someone else to be in full control of my income. This means that I earn my money based off of someone else. It's a very scary place to be, especially when it's your only form of income. This is what I call having a job. There is no freedom in just having a job. Now, I don't think that having a job is bad; it's when you *only* have a job, and nothing else. Be in control of your own income by not leaving all your eggs in one basket.

Have More Free Time

Time is absolutely one of the most valuable assets that you can have. In fact, time is also the one thing you can't get back. I have seen people work, work, work, and work their lives away and when they look back, the one thing they say they would change is that they wish they could have spent more time with their family and friends. I am a true believer in being able to enjoy your time while here on Earth. You unfortunately can't enjoy your time if it's being controlled by only having one stream of income. I have also heard people tell me that they will work hard now and then be able to enjoy their time later in life; however, my belief is that if you can do it now, then why wait?

Be Able to Travel More

To travel the world was always a dream of mine. However, a lot of the places that I always wanted to travel to were very expensive and not the type of trips that could be taken in just a few days. When I only had one stream of income, there was no way I could to afford to travel, let alone even have the time off to do so. Having multiple streams of income has allowed me the freedom to travel the world, and still make money while traveling.

Extra Tax Benefits

A lot of ways to make additional income include direct sales or home businesses, but when you do have a home business, you are given a lot of tax benefits if you live here in the United States. Most items that would be seen as bills can become tax write-offs. A lot of families that I coach actually have home businesses, not just for the additional stream of income, but also so that they can take advantage of the tax benefits. Regardless of how much money you make in the business, you are still given the same benefits. So, yes, you want multiple streams of income because some actually allow you to save money.

You Are Able to Follow Your Passions

What are you passionate about? If you could do anything in the world and money was not an issue, what would it be? Would it be fashion? Would you do missionary work around the world? Would you maybe coach women and men? Whatever it may be, what if you could do it and not worry about how you were able to afford to do it? I have seen a lot of people be able to turn their passion into a business, but also rely solely upon the income from that passion. I tell people all the time to start a business to make money and do your passion to carry out your purpose. When you have multiple streams of income, you are able to do more of the things that

68

drive you. I love spending time with less fortunate children, and I also have two networking groups that I run. One is a networking/training meeting where we show people how to grow their businesses. The other is a women's dinner, where we discuss different challenges that we deal with as women in business and life. I don't make any money doing the things I am passionate about, but it's because I was able to generate multiple streams of real passive income that I am able to spend time helping others. I think that when you are able to carry out your passion in life, that is a true blessing. I also believe that we are all here to be a blessing to someone else.

Start a Stream Today

Now that you know it's a smart idea to have multiple streams of income, the next question is, what should you do? Here are a couple of ideas of how to generate multiple streams of income.

• **Write a book.** For me, being an author has absolutely changed my life. It has been such an incredible journey for me. So much in fact that I totally decided to add a FULL chapter on being an author and why I feel it is truly the path to freedom. I think that for sure if you want to leave a legacy and build multiple streams of income, being an author is the route to go. Please check out my full chapter on being an author and how I can help you get your book done in 72 hours! That's right in fact I have a free gift for you as well to get you started. Go to Bonus.Asixfigurevision.com

- **Taking Paid Surveys at Home.** I was skeptical at first, until my friend's 17-year-old son started making money at home taking paid surveys. Companies desperately want your opinion, and they are willing to pay for it. The trick, of course, is knowing where to find the paid surveys that pay the best. One of the most popular and legitimate survey sites is CashCrate. Not only can you make money taking surveys, but you can also make money by referring friends and family to CashCrate.

- **Start an Online Business.** Making money online requires very little cash investment and can be done on your schedule from home. There are two approaches to getting started. First, you can build a blog. Setting up a blog takes just minutes and costs very little. Join my circle of visionaries group and I will show you how to actually create your own blog for free. It's much easier than you think. Here is someone who actually does online business that you can connect with.

  - **Deric Robinson** Digital Comet Inc digitalcometapps.com

- **Start a coaching business.** There are just so many coaching business opportunities out there. From life coaching to business coaching to career coaching to relationship coaching. Honestly more than ever the coaching industry has grown tremendously. People are starting to understand the importance of investing in self. I always recommend that if you are going to get into the coaching industry just start! Create opportunities for you to work with people and impact them. Coaching can be extremely rewarding. Here are some people who are in different types of coaching industries that you can connect with.

- o **Alexis Ray** Promotional Angles PromotionalAngles.com TheAlexisRay.com
- o **Orlando & Terika Haynes** Coupled For Wealth www.coupledforwealth.com
- o **Lawrence Manifest Gantt** Global Grind Magazine Globalgrindmagazine.com UrbanAmerica.net
- o **Patricia Pearson** Coach Pat LLC coachpatpearson.com
- o **Tara Waggoner** The Tara Waggoner Group taratalk.com
- o **Andrella Pusha** Power and Pathways Consulting AndrellaPusha.com PowerAndPathways.com

- • **Get into The Real Estate Industry.** This is the best time to get into real estate. Regardless of the economy, there will always be a need for professionals in this industry. You'll need an initial investment to obtain your real estate license, but over the long term you'll have the potential to make substantial income. Also, remember that if it's just an additional stream, it's not as stressful.

• **Become a website designer.** With the continued growth of the Internet, website design has become a growing industry. Unless you already have the know-how, you'll need to spend some time learning the technology. But there are plenty of online resources available, and the best in the business can earn a great income. I would also highly recommend outsourcing web design work. The challenge is that you will still need to have knowledge on how to design websites. I actually self-taught myself, and even though it's not my primary source of income, I get a lot of business today from people who need websites designed.

• **Become a Graphic Artist.** There are a lot of ways to generate money through graphics. Just the logo business alone could keep you busy if you have the artistic skills necessary to develop eye catching graphics. Again, this is something that you will need to learn. It can take time but can produce some nice additional income for you.

• **Become a Virtual Assistant.** Virtual assistants today can do just about anything for you without actually requiring a physical presence. Many virtual assistants from places like India or the Philippines are working full time for people in the U.S. The best VA's can earn $30 to $50 per hour. I actually have a VA myself that has been a major asset to my business. The starting place if you are interested in becoming a VA is Elance.com, Odesk.com, or Getafreelancer.com

- **Become a Freelance writer.** If you have a knack for writing, you can earn great money writing for others. Not sure how to start? Contact bloggers who are always looking for great writing. As blogs grow, they can afford to pay freelancers good money for quality articles. Websites looking to build links also hire freelancers to write guest posts to be published on blogs and websites. I found a website, www.freelancewriteruniversity.net, which may be a great resource when learning how to get into this industry. Here is someone that is an author and does writing as an opportunity to earn income.

  o **Latiera N Ford** Book Entitled: Baby Love authorlatieraford.com

- **Start a Home-based business.** The best investment I've ever made was in a home-based business. I strongly recommend that everyone should be in a home-based business. One of the great benefits about running a home business is that it greatly reduces your initial investment. Also, you have a team of individuals to work with. There is usually a system set in place so that it doesn't require a whole lot of creativity on your part. The income opportunities are limitless.

When you look at the extremely wealthy, which consists of the top one percent of income earners in the world, a large number of them have home based businesses. If you are wanting to know of any top home-based businesses to join, simply make sure to join our group for free! There we go over different companies that I recommend that you check out. To join our community simply go to www.showyoursuccessgroup.com. When you join, make sure to introduce yourself. Let us know that you are reading this book! Here are some people that are also in the Home-Based Business industry that I recommend that you can reach out to them.

- **Annette Bryant** Ohenewaa Travel LLC OhenewaaTravel.com TravelSaveMake.com,
- **Elaine Bailey** Nu Home Business Marketing Nuhomebusinessmarketing.com
- **Regina Kenan-Lady Lion'ness** Lady Lion'ness Designs Ladylionnessdesigns.com,
- **Shantell London** MINDSET THERAPY mindsettherapyconsulting.com beatingthegame.info

- **Get into the Health and Wellness Industry.** Believe it or not, there are many ways to join this industry and make great income. Today more people are conscious about their health and wellness more than ever before. People are willing to take those extra precautions to take care of their bodies. You will see that health and wellness products are being promoted

74

everywhere from tv, radio to social media. Health and Wellness products are popping up everywhere. Here are some people that are also in the Health and Wellness Industry, Personal Enrichment, Mental Wellness, Health Care or Insurance that I would recommend that you reach out to.

- o **Charisma DeZonie** The DeZonie Agengy thedezonieagency.com
- o **Constance Mckinsey Neal** Get Healthy Sexy Back gyhsb.com
- o **Lyonezz CANDI** Cultural Arts Natural Design International (CANDI) lyonezzcandi.com
- o **Jewel D. Kitko** Diamond HIT Consult LLC diamondhitconsultllc.com
- o **Queen Vivian Smith-Barnes** IAmQueenViv IAmQueenViv.com
- o **Donnarae Thomas** Calledforareason.com Donnarae.net

- **Sell a product.** I have a good friend who designed a children's clothing line for little boys and is in the process of producing and marketing it. It's a lot of work, but she is passionate about the work, and the potential payoff is huge. Make sure, however, when you decide on what you want to sell, that there is an actual demand for it. I've seen people spend so much time and money on a product, only to find out that the only person who really had a passion for the product was them. Make sure that it's something the market wants.

The best way to do that is to make sure you've done your research.

- **Get into the financial industry.** There are so many different ways in which you can flourish in the financial industry. You can help people learn what to do with their money. You can help people get their credit together. This is truly a growing industry and we are seeing more and more people jump into this industry and make an incredible income. Here is someone that is in the industry.

  - **Lisa Stringer Bailey** Triple M Money Management Matters 7ways2save100shireabookkeeper.info lisastringerbailey.com

- **Become a secret shopper.** I have personally never been a secret shopper, but I do know some people who have done it and have enjoyed it. They go and visit various locations and give feedback to the client about their experiences. It sounds fun and it's a great way to make some money.

- **Become a public speaker.** This is also something that has allowed me to earn multiple six figures from the home-based business industry to now my own coaching and speaking company. Being a great speaker isn't about knowing the biggest words or having the best quotes. I believe the best speakers are the ones who continuously work on developing their skill set. They are themselves and they have a goal to

76

impact other people with their words. Keep in mind, there are different types of speakers. Before you decide to become a speaker, you will want to know exactly what kind of speaker you want to be. Here are some people that are also in the Public Speaking Arena that you can reach out to for help.

   o **Malika Tewari** Seeds To Encourage
   MalikaEncourages.com SeedsToEncourage.com

<u>The different kinds of public speakers are</u>

- **Professional Speakers** - Professional Speakers are hired to present informative content, educate, enthrall, encourage, inspire, and motivate. There are thousands of professional speakers with varying degrees of proficiency and quality.

- **Keynote Speakers** - Speakers who talk for approximately one hour at a general session, dinner, or banquet on any subject of which you can conceive. Keynote Speakers fall into a variety of subcategories: Motivational Speakers, Inspirational Speakers, Educational Speakers, and Celebrity Speakers.

- **Seminar Leaders** - Any expert on a particular topic or subject whose objective is to educate and or motivate. Their delivery is usually more conversational than that of the Keynoter—with a longer format that allows more interaction between the presenter and the audience.

- **Workshop Facilitators** - Similar to teachers in a school, these presenters usually work with smaller audiences—which allows for more individual attention. The facilitator can provide guidance as participants practice using newly acquired knowledge and understanding skills.

- **Trainers** - They are workshop facilitators who specialize in hands-on training of a specific skill—which will later be used by the participants in their work. Generally, trainers are hired to train employees at the organization's own facility and only occasionally at a meeting or convention.

- **Industry Speakers** - These are speakers with expertise or a reputation in a particular industry or field. The specific information they impart is usually of special value only to a particular audience. For example, a popular industry would be marketing.

- **The Entertainer** - They are used mostly for general sessions, dinners, banquets, parties and special events. These can be humorists, comedians, mentalists, hypnotists, skit and industrial show actors, jugglers, dancers, variety acts, musical attractions and whatever else the mind can conceive of. The Categories are endless.

- **The Combination Program** - There are a handful of professional entertainers who are also excellent professional speakers. These few not only entertain an audience but can also educate them—interweaving a powerful and motivating message that can make the difference between a successful meeting and a great one.

Sidenote: Yes, I also help people develop talks that sell. To learn more about this make sure you have downloaded the bonuses. I will send you a free training on making six figures as a public speaker. Speaking to groups of people is truly what has allowed me now to do millions in sales! I look forward to helping you do the same.

Chapter 6: Mentorship

"A mentor is someone who allows you to see the hope inside yourself. A mentor is someone who allows you to know that no matter how dark the night, in the morning joy will come. A mentor is someone who allows you to see the higher part of yourself when sometimes it becomes hidden to your own view."

Oprah Winfrey

Mentorship

What is a Mentor?

Mentoring is most often defined as a relationship in which an experienced person (the mentor) assists another (the mentee) in developing specific skills and knowledge that will enhance the less-experienced person's professional, spiritual, physical, and/or personal growth. Having a mentor has absolutely changed my life, and it's because of having my mentor every step of the way, that I believe the way I do. You must be willing to trust your mentor, even if you don't understand their instruction. Your mentor focuses on your future, not your past. They allow you to learn through their experiences instead of your mistakes. With the help of a great mentor, your path to freedom will be much shorter than if you didn't have one. In fact, it would almost be impossible to do anything new and different alone. Don't look for your mentor to tell you what you do right, but what you do wrong. They aren't there to justify your failures and/or ignore your flaws. Your mentor will not be afraid to call you out. You can't be afraid to receive your corrections or get defensive. I have had several individuals in my past coaching experiences that wanted me to mentor them, but mentoring is not for everyone. You have to be ready to be taken apart and then put back together. One of the best

82

investments you can ever make in life is spending time with your mentor.

A Coach vs. A Mentor

I have coached thousands but mentored only a handful of people. There is a big difference between the two. Your mentor may be your coach, but your coach doesn't necessarily have to be your mentor. I describe a little of what it means to be coached, but when it comes to mentoring, your mentor will be more engaged in the details of your everyday life that may affect that area they are mentoring you in. I have had four different mentors so far, and they know a lot about me personally. You may even have a mentor who doesn't know you at all, but you follow their teachings. However, having those personal relationships allowed my mentors to better help me, because they actually knew me as a person.

Mentors Have Great Qualities

A mentor should have the qualities about them that you wish to possess. They should inspire you to want to be better and to want more. I am so grateful for my mentors because they never stayed who they were. That meant I could never get comfortable where I was in life.

Mentors Have Wisdom

There are two ways you learn in life. You either learn from your mistakes or you can learn from the wisdom of someone else, who has already gone through those mistakes. I had the hardest time in growth when I didn't have someone helping me. I would make mistakes, and even though I learned from them, I found that when my mentor would help me based off their experiences, it took far less time to obtain the goal I had set. Wisdom comes from experience, and I would rather save time and learn from someone who has already walked down that road than to walk down it myself.

Mentors Give You Additional Perspective

I appreciate the fact that my mentor was always able to help me in my decision-making process. Your mentor will more than likely not always see eye-to-eye on everything with you, but that's to be expected. If you saw eye-to-eye all the time, there would be no need for you to have a mentor. A lot of times when I was thinking about doing something one way, my mentor saw a different perspective and I was able to go at it in a different way and produce amazing results. You never want to leave your major ideas to yourself. Your mentor will be able to make sure you see the bigger picture, or even if there are alternative routes to helping you toward your freedom.

84

Your Mentor Isn't Your Best Friend

Your best friend loves you the way you are, but your mentor loves you too much to leave you the way you are. Your mentor will push you and not be afraid to push your buttons if it means getting you to succeed. Your mentor will not let you stay comfortable, while your best friend will allow you to do what you want. Be grateful that your mentor believes in you so much that they won't allow you to stay where you are.

Mentors are your Personal Coach not your Cheerleader

The difference between the two is that a cheerleader will cheer for you regardless of if you are winning or losing. When you think about a game, cheerleaders cheer regardless of the score, are there to keep a smile on your face and don't really affect the outcome of the game. When you look at the coach, it's a totally different situation. If you make a mistake on the court or field, they will correct you. They will change the plays. They might even push you until you become uncomfortable. The reason you have a mentor is not just for support, but also for change. If you want freedom, you need someone who is committed to showing you how to get it. I will also say that most people would rather have a cheerleader than a coach, but if you are serious about freedom, then you must have someone who is not afraid to push you.

Mentors Help You Set Goals

I was very ignorant about setting goals. So ignorant that the six steps for setting goals I went over in the earlier chapter, were incredibly difficult for me to follow. I never knew how important it was to set goals. I never knew why I wasn't completing anything that I had set out to accomplish in life. It was my mentor who showed me how to properly set goals, and because my mentor was also my coach, they kept me accountable for working toward my goals. Goal setting is very important, but you also want to have someone whom you can safely share and work on your goals with. That's the job of your mentor.

Mentors Provide Accountability

Everyone needs an accountability partner. This is someone who will hold you accountable for obtaining your goals; someone who won't allow your excuses to keep you from your success. I found that my mentor was my most valuable accountability partner because most of all, I never wanted to let them down. I was able to focus because I knew that when I sat down with my mentor to discuss my growth, they wouldn't allow failure to be an option. My mentor would always encourage me to see the greatness in myself through words, and because of that, I also allowed them to hold me accountable for carrying out that greatness. Never choose an accountability partner who doesn't express the same interests as you do. In most cases, because your mentor has already accomplished what it is that you want, they are the best qualified at holding you to your goals.

Mentors Think Outside The Box

"If you always do what you always did, you will always get what you always got." -Albert Einstein

Unfortunately, one of my biggest challenges was trying to express my ideas and future with my friends and family. I remember that one of my friends actually told me that I should just stay working my job instead of going after my vision of freedom. Fortunately for me, my mentor came into my life and allowed me to think outside the box. When you ask someone why they go to work, they will more than likely tell you it's because they need to pay the bills. That's what all people believe, but that's inside-the-box thinking. Remember, your mentor has what it is that you want, so they will challenge you at times. They will force you to change your ways of thinking. Thinking outside the box is what has allowed me to change my circumstance.

How to Find a Mentor

Now that you understand why you need a mentor; the next step is to actually find a mentor. A mentor should be someone in that area of interest that has what it is you desire. My spiritual mentor is my pastor. My business mentor is also a part of my home business and has become a mult-millionaire in the company. My relationship mentor is also a relationship expert, who has helped hundreds of families all over the world. My fitness mentor is my trainer. I don't have a single mentor who covers all areas of my life, but I am blessed to have all areas of my life covered. The best place to find your mentor is, of course, in that arena. Make sure this is a person who you want to be like. Someone whose shoes you would want to walk in based on what you see, and they will be the person to help you through the journey that you don't see. Also keep in mind that your mentor may not always be someone that you personally know. For example, I don't have relationship with my spiritual mentor. He is able to mentor me every Sunday and Wednesday at church. I also read a lot of his books. I follow his teachings. So even though I don't have that personal talking relationship, he has been able to strengthen me spiritually. You may not meet all your mentors. If you need help with finding a mentor, be sure to visit our website www.showyoursuccess.com. There we list mentors and coaches in different areas of your life.

Chapter 7: Change Your Circle

"Be careful the environment you choose for it will shape you; be careful the friends you choose for you will become like them."

W. Clement Stone

There Will Be a Season of Separation

When you make a decision to go after your goals and vision to freedom, you will face opposition from those individuals you've spent a lot of your time with. One of the most challenging decisions that I ever had to make was to take time away from people that I loved. I needed to take time to work on myself. For some people, it was a permanent separation, while others were only temporary. One of the things that I also noticed was that I started spending more time with loved ones who I no longer shared interests with, and some of my friends and family noticed, too. Some were inspired to do more. It is an awesome feeling to help others by leading by example. I tell people all the time that the season of separation doesn't have to be forever, but if your friends and family really love you, they will understand. You will also help inspire them based off of your results. I find that more people get inspired by my results, not my words or actions.

Birds of a Feather Flock Together

Have you ever noticed that sometimes when you're around a negative person, you start talking negative? Or when you are around someone happy, you feel happy? Whomever you choose to converse with will ultimately affect you and

90

your disposition. I have to say this multiple times because it's so important that when you set your vision to freedom, you will be going against the grain of probably most of the people in your circle, and you will need to make a decision about what's more important. You become what you think about. Words affect your thoughts, and your thoughts affect your words. This is also why I don't watch the news. You might even find that you have to live like an eagle. You might have to fly alone in most cases. They say the top is lonely, but the truth is that it really isn't; it's just that so many people would rather be at the bottom. It can be scary climbing that mountain to freedom.

One thing I will also add is that your real friends will be inspired by you and also start having a vision. They may not want to do what you do, but they will be inspired to do other things instead of the norm. That's when you know that your results have really started to show in life. I get so inspired when my friends start ventures on their own. Also keep in mind that there are sometimes when the circle may even change for the better, but ultimately not everyone will come with you on your journey to freedom.

Your Circle of Influence will Increase Your Quality of Life

I noticed that when I started changing my circle, my life started to change instantly. I started being invited to so many events I never knew existed. I found myself joining private clubs of the elite. I learned about all these different ways to make money. These circles always helped me grow in whatever I was doing. It became easier because everyone was so positive. The circles never discussed things like being broke, sad, or sick. Instead, they talked about investing, trips, cars, etc. One of the other great things was that once I got in the circle, I was able invite some of my other friends into the circle too - the friends, of course, who had vision.

Your Beliefs are Affected by Your Circle of Influence

People who you surround yourself with all have beliefs that can impact your life. Whenever you allow someone to speak to you, regardless if you think you believe what they are saying or not, you will eventually start to believe them. The more you allow their words to breathe life into your mind, the sooner they will start to affect you. Be careful who you let speak life into you. If someone in my circle is always negative, eventually it would make me negative as well. I had to make sure at the beginning of my journey to be very careful with whom I spoke with. Some people would get a limit of an hour, a few minutes, or no time at all.

Surround Yourself with Your Future Not Your Past

Put yourself in the environment to be around people you want to be like, and eventually you'll start to be like them. I've always believed that I should never be the smartest person in my circle. I never wanted to have the most money, either. I continue to want to be challenged, and what I love so much about my primary means of income is that my circle constantly out-earns and outgrows me. Because of this, I am never allowed to stay comfortable at my current level of success. Surround yourself as much as possible with people who inspire you. Even if you don't get to talk to them, just watch them. It will impact you. You'll notice that they will eventually start speaking to you. Once you build a relationship with someone, you will also find they will connect you to many other people and opportunities.

Join a Mastermind Group

To most people, the idea of a mastermind groups is fairly new. However, mastermind groups have been around forever. Napoleon Hill, author of "Think and Grow Rich," actually had his own mastermind group while writing the book. A mastermind group is designed to help you navigate through challenges using the collective intelligence of others.

Mastermind groups typically meet either weekly, monthly or daily, depending on what makes sense regarding the purpose and plan for the group. Individuals in your mastermind group should be able to lean on each other, give advice, and share connections. You may have people in different businesses apart from this group and you are able to do business with each other. It's sort of a form of peer-to-peer mentoring. If you get invited to join an effective mastermind group, you will most definitely see a change in yourself and your business. You can also form a group of your own.

Here are 7 reasons why you should be in a mastermind group:

1. **You'll be part of an exclusive community.** In most cases, to be in a mastermind group means you were invited. You will be able to feed off of other individual's strengths where you may be weak.

2. **You aren't alone.** You are able to now have a group of people who share your vision. They may not be in the exact business structure or industry, but they have the ultimate vision of freedom and you can relate. This helps you to not feel alone.

3. **Advisement.** The other members of the group turn into business advisors of sorts, and vice versa. Two minds are

94

always greater than one. To get ideas from others is always helpful.

4.   **Collaboration is the name of the game.** You'll start to find out that other people in your group may be able to assist you in a project. The group works together collaboratively, to achieve more together.

5.   **Extend your network.** I believe fully that your net-worth is determined by your network. So, when you join a mastermind group, you also expand your network exponentially and rapidly. If you are in business, you know how important your network is. By joining a mastermind group, you instantly add to your network and typically gain the networks of those in the group with you.

6.   **Cross-promotion.** When you join a mastermind group, be sure to find a group where you all are able to help each other in promotion. You can use a service of someone in your mastermind group in exchange of your service. Also, you're able to connect those in your mastermind group to other people you may know who would need their services.

7.   **New learning and bigger thinking.** Joining a mastermind group helped me so much in business because I was also able to learn other amazing strategies in growing my business, and as a result of learning theses skills, I also was

able to think even bigger. You can't help but think bigger and stretch beyond your boundaries when surrounded by amazing people doing amazing things.

Your mastermind group doesn't replace your need to have a mentor, but they will bring added value to your life. Masterminds are incredible and can-do wonders for your business as well as for you, personally. Growing in a group is not only more effective, it's quite a bit more fun!

Stop Caring What Others Think About You

What other people think about you is none of your business. It's their business. Wasting your time thinking about what they are thinking about you serves nothing. Seeking approval is a waste of your time and energy. It will only bring you suffering. It's not about whether others approve of you, but that you approve of yourself. This is what counts. I remember being at an event, and a leader was talking about the average funeral. He said that at the average funeral, only 10 people will cry for you. Half of the group will come to your burial, and if it's raining, only half of the half will come. When I heard that, I immediately understood how I, for so long, worried about what people thought of me –and now to think they wouldn't even come to my funeral! I learned quickly to stop focusing on what everyone else thought, and just focused on where I was going. I also remember that during some of the most challenging times in my life, there were only a handful of people who stuck in there with me. In life, you must understand ultimately that this is your life and you are responsible for the outcome of it. No one else is responsible for your success. So, don't waste your time worrying about someone who isn't worrying about you.

When you put yourself out there in the world and dare to follow your dreams and vision to freedom, it is a risk. It is a vulnerable and courageous act. People will judge you. People will talk about you. People will project their stuff onto you. Some people are even afraid you will leave them. In fact, some people simply won't like you, and they may not even know you! This is unavoidable. Jesus was perfect. He was the only perfect human being in the world. He simply wanted the best for people, and people still hated him. Make peace with this up front. Do not give those who don't even know you the power to determine your happiness. Do not give even those who do know you the power to determine who you should be and what your limits are. Trust in your vision and know who you are. As you accept yourself as you are and as you are not, you become powerful. You consolidate your energy and remain rooted in your center. You become free. When you no longer seek other people's approval, you are free. As you unhook yourself from other people's validation, you become truly powerful.

When I think about a completely free person, I think of children. They are so free and they don't care about what other people think. There unfortunately comes a point in their life when they stop being silly and crazy. I remember one time I was on a plane flying somewhere, and this little baby who was sitting in front of me jumped up and turned around and just stared at me. I mean, a full beam, no blinking, weird uncomfortable stare. I said hello to him, but no answer. He just stared at me. He didn't care what I thought. He didn't care what anyone else thought. No one stopped him, either. He just stared. That's when I had my "ah hah!" moment. I would spend time watching children and how they interacted. They were just so free. However, what was also most interesting was that they were so very happy. It's not until we learn that through life that we should be conscious of what other people think of us.

I want to leave you with this prayer because this is a tough chapter. I know because it was hard to separate myself from people who I loved. However, I loved them so much that I knew that my life had to change. I couldn't stay in the same circumstance that I was in to be able to help them. Learn to let go of those things you can't control. You can only control you, your thoughts, your words, your actions. It's about you. Whenever I found myself stuck in a place of question, I would speak this prayer.

Serenity Prayer

God grant me the serenity to accept the things I cannot change; courage to change the things I can; and wisdom to know the difference.

Chapter 8: Leave a Legacy with a Book

"Don't let what you don't know scare you, because it can become your greatest asset. And if you do things without knowing how they have always been done, you're guaranteed to do them differently."

Sara Blakely

Well first of all congratulations on getting a copy of this free e-book where you're going to learn the reasons why I believe that every business owner should write a book. Today when you think about competition in the business world it is continuing to increase every single day. With 28 million registered businesses in the United States as well as 20 million entrepreneurs and network marketing, the competition is most definitely getting stiff. You must find ways to absolutely stand out if you plan on being noticed. Now one thing I will say about myself is that I do not believe in competition. I do believe in creation however at the end of the day you must still stand out in order to connect with those who are ordained for you. It is so important that you are doing all that you can so that you can stand out in this crowded world. Not only does being an author help you do that, but it can also help bring in so many additional benefits. In this e-book, you're going to learn 6 reasons why I totally believe that you need to get your book done and not next year but within the next 30 days. I promise you this being an author is absolutely the way to go. Enjoy the next few pages and once you are done make sure that you reach out to me so you can learn how to get started on your book today!

It's Better Than a Business Card

When you think about a business card, you think about the traditional 2.5 X 5 size card that every single person gets and simply puts away in a drawer full of other business cards. Let's just be real, this technique of passing business cards to other people doesn't really work. I have a serious question for you... When was the last time somebody actually called you and said hey I found your business card and I want to be able to get you to come and speak to my organization about XY and Z? The answer to that is going to be very slim to none.

Let's be honest business cards can really just be a waste of space. Every now and then yes you might be able to get a lead from passing your card out but one thing that I do know that will leave a forever Lasting Impression is the fact that you are an author. One thing that I have used more than anything is my book to get me in front of the most influential people in my industry. It is something that people will never throw away nor will they put in a box of other cards. When you think about having a book it is really simply a business card on steroids. Yes, it's going to be a little bit more expensive and that is why I do not recommend just giving it to everyone however a book can most definitely Lead You In the doors to the right person. The best business card around in my opinion.

It builds Your Credibility

Being an author changed my life and business immediately. I never before in my life found it so easy to get in front of a group of people and credible outlets like Fox News, CBS & ABC until I wrote a a book. Writing a book makes you the expert. It doesn't matter if you have a degree or ANYTHING. People assume the fact that you are an author, you know what you are talking about.

I've never ever been asked how long I've been goal setting or coaching or speaking. The fact that I have a book has really put me in a position where no one questions what I speak on. The fact that I wrote about "it" then I know about it. It is an instant credibility builder. Now what I will say is make sure that you do know what you wrote about. LOL because hopefully you will then be offered an opportunity to speak on that of what you've written about.

People Love to Hire Authors

PEOPLE LOVE TO HIRE AUTHORS. PEOPLE LOVE TO HIGHLIGHT AUTHORS. PEOPLE WANT TO WRITE STORIES ABOUT AUTHORS. If you are looking for ways to get on the news, magazines, newspapers and more, then you should most definitely write a book. Today more than ever, media outlets are always looking for stories to highlight. One of the easiest ways to get a story done on you, is to write a book about a topic that people want to hear about. When you write a book, it makes it so much easier to market what you are selling. Also keep in mind books are the easiest things to sell.

One tip I would give about what topic to write your book on is in one of the industries of health & wellness (weight loss), success (finances) and/or love.

One thing you must also keep in mind is the once your book is done, you must also be willing to roll your sleeves up and get in front of people. Most people think that if you write a book then automatically the doors will open. The truth is it makes it easier to

market yourself BUT you must STILL market yourself.

One of the KEY things I love coaching on is HOW to market your book! Let me help you out!

It can win you business

The truth is this... There are YES a lot of authors in the world but within your specific industry... NO! If you want to win the business, be the influencer. The influencer is the author. It is really as simple as that. One of the tips I always teach my students is to use your book to open up doors. I have used my book as a way to do some incredible things in business.

There have been opportunities where I know for a fact that someone was looking for speakers and because I was the "author" I was more attractive. The truth is this... If you are an author AGAIN it makes you more attractive in the market.

Please keep in mind.. To win the business you must raise your hand. You must get in front of people. You must be willing to let those with the opportunities know that you are there. You will be surprised how your book will win you so many opportunities if you know how to properly leverage your book.

Leaves a Legacy for Your Family

If it is one thing that I hear from a lot of entrepreneurs, is it they want to leave a legacy for their family. Writing a book is the one true way in which you can do so without really having to make millions of dollars before it is done.

I had an opportunity to sit down with a bishop of many churches in Georgia. He was sharing with me a book that he was working on. The book was written by his mother who had passed away but left him the electronic version of her book. She left him the opportunity to work on her book and republish it with his name. Long after we are all gone, our books will still be here. We're talking about an opportunity for our books to be found in the hands of generations after generations after generations. What better way to leave a legacy then to leave your value, your experience, your journey to the world.

There are things that you know how to do TODAY that you can share with the world and impact people in a major way.

It can make you multiple streams of income

This is absolutely one of my favorite reasons for writing a book and that is multiple streams of income. One of the gifts that I believe I have is to be able to show somebody what it is that they currently do and how to turn that into multiple streams of income. When you think about our lives, we have multiple bills. Why not make multiple streams of income as well? A lot of times we are leaving so much money on the table because we are only focused on our high-ticket item that we sell. Whatever that may be regardless if it is a service or a product, there are always ways to make multiple streams of income with your current business.

I believe a book can at least make you 3 sturdy streams which can increase too many different ways depending upon what kind of business you are in. However, I can guarantee you that 3 with your book to get you started. The average millionaire has at least seven streams of income so if you write your book then that means you're halfway there. Your book of course is going to be 1 stream but then you are able to turn that into additional ways including "info" information and more to build your business. I would love to be able to work with you and

show you how to take your business and your book and turn it into multiple streams of income. In the conclusion I will give you some additional ways of how we can make that happen but focus on how you can take your book and turn it into multiple streams of

income. You can also sell things within. your book. A little tip is to never mention the name of a product that you do not own but use a website redirect to send your readers to.

Chapter 9: Personal Development

"The greatest battle you will ever face will be the transformation of you."

Edward Hartley

Personal Development

I've always been told that the size of your library will also determine your income. Whatever it is that you have decided freedom means to you, you have to develop your mind. One of the first things that my mentor recommended was to work on developing who I wanted to become. I had to work on my mind more than anything else, because it's your mind that determines who you are. I started investing a lot of money into myself. I attended events, read books, and listened to audios.

Personal development is important because it will help you in prioritizing the important things in life, it increases your mental capacity and it will connect you to positive people. Ignoring personal development will make you stagnant in life.

Personal Development Raises Awareness

The reason most people go through life being negative or feeling sad is because they haven't been made aware that they are in control of their thoughts and feelings. I didn't know this before I started to develop myself. I didn't know that my words were so powerful. Even though I believed the world was created with words, I was never taught to be conscious of *my* words. I even realized that there were certain situations where I used the law of attraction and didn't even know it.

Personal Development will Build Your Confidence

I used to believe I was shy, but then I realized that it was just a belief someone else had instilled in me. I used to believe I was shy, because others told me I was; the more I heard it, the more I believed it, the more I became it. I started to read books on building my confidence. I read about other people who were just like me that were able to change, and that gave me strength. I started learning how to visualize who I wanted to become. I still do it to this day. I just see myself growing which gives me further confidence of who I will become.

Become a Doer Not Just a Reader

Now that you are aware of personal development, I want to warn you of the Personal Development Junkies. There are some individuals who you will find have a lot of information, but no activity. In fact, it has been found that only about 10% of the world actually buys into personal development. However, less than 10% of that 10% take that knowledge into action.

If you ask me, personal development is not just about acquiring new information, but about developing new skills and attitudes. However, developing skills and attitudes requires practice. It means a whole lot of practice; taking massive action, being organized, consistent and persistent. Also remember it took you however old you are to become who you are today, so to develop into that woman or man isn't going to happen overnight.

Most people I know who get into the reading part - considering how much they actually need to practice to turn the knowledge into skills and attitudes, just the most valuable knowledge - they barely scratch the surface.

They read a good book, find some very valuable and practical ideas, they even start applying them for a few days, and then they move on to the next book, seeking some new "inspiration." They are the "readers." I call it broken focus.

I used to do this until I discovered I was just being a personal development literature enjoyer. Some people read love novels; I read "As a Man/Woman Thinketh" and the likes. I still enjoy the reading part a lot, but I'm very aware that this is not what real self-improvement is mainly about, so I also focus a lot on practicing what I read; on being a "doer."

Besides the difference of obviously applying what you have learned through your readings, audios, or events, there are three important differences I also believe when it comes to a personal development reader versus a doer.

112

Doers focus on selecting, remembering and organizing the most valuable personal development ideas from what they read and they put them into their growth plan. My mentor would always say it's not about learning the whole book or audio, it's about finding a chapter or section that you identify with and study it and apply it.

Doers use strategies for doing, they set practice goals and daily practice tasks; they keep track of progress and find ways to keep themselves motivated. They make sure to also stay in council with their mentor about what to read that relates to their goals and vision to freedom.

Doers sometime consciously cut down their reading, as they understand that new information can often interfere with their practicing and defocus them from their goals. Rather, they sometimes re-read the stuff they're already applying, to keep themselves going. There are some books that I read over and over. When I think of a book like "Think and Grow Rich" from Napoleon Hill, it seems like every time I read it, I learn something different to apply to my life. It's not about having 'read' or 'heard' but about 'reading' and 'hearing.'

The result is the actual growing process as a person. I think you can often separate the doers from the readers because the doers are the ones you see after two or three years and they seem strikingly changed, improved; maybe they're more confident, happier, more expressive, more charming or simply... richer. I don't know about you, but I for one have the pleasure of knowing only about a handful of people such as these.

Personal Development Shows You How to Change

You must be willing to take action. I've spent a lot of money attending conferences to see some of the best speakers in the world. I would always wonder how could so many people attend these events, but not see the results. Most people want the change but aren't willing to go after it. Your willingness to change must be greater than your willingness to learn. That's the first step. Then you must also be able to take the proper action steps. You can't take on the whole world at one time. Be gradual. Set your goals and stay in constant communication with your mentor.

Developing Yourself Will Help Others

Now that you are working on you, you will start to help others. I made it a habit to work harder on me than anybody else, and when I did that, my growth would automatically start to spread to others. I knew it was working when I would start having people ask me what I did for a living. They would tell me that I just looked happy, and that they wanted to be happy, too. It wasn't always about my materialistic possessions, but

114

the positive energy that I would give off. Through my own growth, I have had so many great things happen that have changed in my life for the better, and because of that, I have been able to inspire other people through my words. I now have made it my personal goal to impact the lives of over 1,000,000 men and women through my words and actions.

Personal Development Will Increase Your Potential

When you start working on you, others will notice your growth. I have seen people strengthen their relationships with their friends, family, and significant others. I have seen people get promotions at their jobs. I've seen people's lives change instantly because of who they started to become. They started attracting so many great things to their life. Your potential in life will increase extremely if you continue to work on you more than anything else. I am so grateful for a young lady who actually introduced me to the world of personal development. In fact, the first international speaker I ever saw was Dani Johnson. Once I saw her, I was so inspired to change my life. It honestly was the beginning of my journey, and because of who I am becoming, I know that I can do whatever I desire.

You Must Work on Yourself Every Day

Personal development is not a one-time deal. You must be willing to work on yourself every day. I take time every single day to listen to personal development audio for at least 30 minutes. I also read every day. Constantly strengthening your mind is vital when it comes to growth. You'll find in life that you'll never arrive to a final place, but you are always becoming a new and better person. Do it every day! Don't miss a single day! You can't afford to when you have so many things that are about to happen in your life.

Learn to Have Focused Attention

When you take the time to work on your personal development, be sure not to have any other distractions. I see it all the time: someone will have an audio playing, but at the same time, they're on their phone. How can you possibly be learning when your mind is being consumed with other words and information that you are in control of? I use my car for listening to audio. My car has become a library on wheels, and people know when they get in my car, they need to be quiet if something related to personal development is playing on the radio. When reading, find a quiet place where you won't be distracted so you will be able to give your full attention to what you are reading.

Always Take Notes

If you ever attend an event where the person who is speaking is where you want to be in life, take notes. When you don't take notes, you will likely forget more than 90% of the information. I keep a journal for taking notes and recording ideas and have made it a habit to review my journal at least once every week.

Take Personal Development Serious

Personal development is serious, but because so few people do it, don't be surprised if some people don't agree with what you are learning. However, don't let that affect you. Take this seriously. Your capacity to learn and take action is everything when it comes to your journey to freedom. Do it every day and never give up. Focus on your words, what you see and read, and how you feel. Make sure to put money aside to invest more and more into your growth. Personal development is not something you do once. It will become a part of your everyday life.

Want to Know Where to Start?

I would say that personal development is specific as well. You will want to read something that will help you grow in the area of your life that you need growth. There are several books and audios that I would recommend; however, it's also important that you seek council with your mentor. Your mentor will know more about you personally and be able to better recommend what will work best for you. To see some of the books I recommend, visit my website at: www.ShowYourSuccess.com. I have some free books and audio that I give away, and I also recommend some that you can buy. Of course, this book, "A Six Figure Vision," is a great start - so good for you!

Chapter 10: Stay Patient in The Process

"If you stay patient with the seed, the harvest will always follow"

Taurea V Avant

Your Time is Coming

This journey that you are about to embark on will take time. It took you however old you are today to become the person you are today, so make sure to remember to always stay patient with the process. Sometimes what I see with a lot of my students is that they are so excited about where they are going, they forget about the journey. I hear things like, "I just want it to happen now!" In a perfect world, things would work out that way; however, in *this world*, you must also understand that everything will happen in time. You must never disrespect the journey that you have to go through to get to the other side. There is no test without the testimony. There is not victory before the battle. However, also remember that God will never put more on you than you can bear. I love the idea of challenges as well, because when a challenge arrives, I know I'm that much closer to achieving my goal.

Focus on the End in Mind

When you go through challenges in life, one of the things I recommend is to always focus on the end in mind. Of course, still respect the journey by going through the journey, but keep your eye focused on where you will end up. Don't worry about how you will do everything. What has always happened to me is that even though many times I didn't know how I would achieve my goals, everything always worked itself out. This will happen for you as well. Don't allow anyone to break your focus. One of my favorite things to say to my students is "There is no room for broken focus". If your dream of freedom is big enough, you can't allow anything to throw you off course.

You Can Only Control Your Actions

Also remember that when it comes to going after your goals, the only things you can really control are your thinking and your actions. You don't have the power to make anyone do anything. You can inspire people, but you can't make people do anything they aren't willing to do. So keep this in mind. Don't allow people to frustrate you. Don't allow someone else not believing in your vision ruin your mood. I learned very quickly to believe in people, but not always believe people. I knew that I was to really going to make things happen, I would have to lead by example.

Keep a Journal

One of the things my mentor would always talk to me about was keeping a "what am I doing right" journal. In this journal I would briefly describe what I did in that day; what I had accomplished. Sometimes I even wrote what I wore and how I was feeling. Writing in my journal allowed me to stay patient with the process because I could see the progress. Get yourself a journal today! I will also be doing teleseminars on journal writing and how it can truly help you in your journey to freedom. Be sure to join me on some of them!

Always remember that you will eventually get what you want

This requires maturity and patience to understand and accept! If you work hard at something, this may be the truth, but most of the time you have to be patient to get what you want. For others, this may come more easily, but the only thing that matters is that you know how to occupy yourself, even in the dead of times.

Just remember, patience is a mental skill that you will never forget, so cherish patience as a major step for you in life. Impatience is something not to be proud of, but something that you should attempt to train yourself out of, before it is something that overthrows your life.

Think about the People You will Impact

When I think of freedom, true freedom to me is when I can help other people to obtain freedom as well. This is what really allowed me to have an amazing amount of patience in my journey toward freedom.

You can get anything you want out of life when you help others to get what they want. I learned that from the great Zig

Ziglar. I have made it a mission to impact the lives of other people through what I have been able to learn in life. I think about the story of the average funeral, and I know that I won't go out like that.

When it's all said and done and they write about my life, I will be remembered as a woman who changed lives all over the world. Hundreds will come and thousands will watch and millions will know about the legacy I leave when we have that final day to celebrate the life I lived. If I help one person to make a major impact on someone else's life, then I know I've done my due diligence, but I know that has already been done. I get excited when I think about the people that I will help from my story. When my father passed away, I had a paradigm shift about life. I realized that in life, people don't remember you for the things you owned, but for who you impacted. I look forward to impacting your life.

Chapter 11: Get Started Today

"Remember, a real decision is measured by the fact that you've taken new action. If there's no action, you haven't truly decided."

Anthony Robbins

Get Started Today

Congratulations! You have finished the book and I want you to know how truly proud I am of you. You have done what only 2% of the population will do, and that's invest in your personal development. Now the challenge is taking the action steps towards your freedom.

I didn't write this book because I want you to know this information. I wrote this book because I want you to *do* this information. I'm always telling my students that I don't want you to just talk about it; I want you to walk it out. Start practicing the advice in this book today. Invest in more self-education. Study what people who are free according to your definition do and study what people who are not free do. Follow the advice of the people that can help you get to your next level in life.

When you start to follow these steps, you will see an almost immediate impact on your life. You'll start to see your finances change, your health change, and your circle change for the better. You'll be able to start doing more of the things you enjoy and less of the things you hate.

But let's keep first things first. Talk with the person who gave you this book and ask them what it is that they do for a living. Ask them if they can help you to go after freedom.

You are also welcome to contact our office and we will connect you with a mentor who can assist you in starting your journey to freedom today.

Also, don't forget about the bonuses I have for you for buying this book! Go to **Bonus.Asixfigurevision.com** and make sure you also join our Show Your Success Group by going to **www.ShowYourSuccessGroup.com**. In my group, you will be able to join me for tons of training and opportunities to work with me one-on-one.

BY THE WAY.... Did you know about the audio that also comes with some additional bonuses? YES!!! Grab a copy of the audio by going to **Audio.ASixFigureVision.com** TODAY!

About the Author

Taurea Vision Avant started off in life with the vision of the American Dream: going to college, getting good grades, graduating and then going off to work in Corporate America. Unfortunately, after she graduated with a bachelor's degree in Computer Science from Hampton University, she went from temp job to temp job to temp job. It didn't look like her dream of landing a career job in her degree was going to happen. Finally, she landed a small salaried job as a database administrator - which is just a fancy name for data entry. Even with the salaried job, she still lived paycheck to paycheck, barely making it. Can you relate?

Then the turning point in Taurea's life happened. It's what you call a "paradigm shift" (A lot of us have major turning points that will require a major shift to take place.... When will your shift occur, or has it already?).

Her father, her hero, her last living parent was diagnosed with stage 4 lung cancer October of 2006. Her mother had passed away when she was just 12 years old due to cirrhosis of the liver, so this news totally turned her life upside down. She found herself in a place of loneliness and completely lost. She had to watch her father go through this disease and ultimately be defeated. One thing that stayed with her was the thought: Did her father seize the opportunity to do everything he wanted in life? Did he make excuses on why he couldn't do something like so many of us do? Did he lose his will to dream? She vowed from then on to not let this happen to her.

She moved to Atlanta, Ga in August of 2007 in hopes of starting her own business in multimedia. Unfortunately, long story short, it failed. She had invested $40,000 into the business and it turned into her making $800 in 2008. However, "We know that the most successful people in the world have failed the most on their journey to success," so she never let that hold her back. Most of us would have given up. If it weren't for failing, we wouldn't know of Henry Ford, Bill Gates, Walt Disney, Albert Einstein, Socrates, Oprah Winfrey, or Michael Jordan… JUST TO NAME A FEW!

Taurea went from Foreclosure in 2009 to producing millions in sales in the home-based business industry. She is the creator of The System Mastery and Show Your Success Workshops, and 15+ Time Author of books on personal self-development, education and more. Her major focus is to show entrepreneurs how to build multiple streams of income in their current businesses She has been seen on Fox News, CBS News, ABC News, Sheen Magazine, Successful Women Radio Show, IHeartRadio and more!

Taurea's focus is on helping small-based business owners & independent distributors to develop, master, and remain committed to growing their businesses by providing valuable leadership and interpersonal skills. She offers timeless tips that support in real world interactions and discoveries on what it takes to be successful in today's entrepreneurial world. She is a living example of creating a lifetime career and wants to help you get prepared for the journey. She knows what it takes to break through a multitude of challenges and focus on the future.

Today, Taurea has been able to generate multiple streams of income, but her true passion is being able to empower women and men all over the world. Her true mission in life is to impact the lives of 10,000,000 men and women around the world.

She believes that in life, "People don't remember you for the clothes you wore, the cars you drove, or the jewelry you owned. They only remember you for the impact that you had on other people's lives." That is her true mission in life!

More on Taurea Avant

To have Taurea Vision Avant speak to your organization about the principles found in A Six Figure Vision or other success insights, e-mail speakerrequest@taureaavant.com or go to her website www.TaureaAvant.com

Made in the USA
Middletown, DE
10 May 2022

65546516R00075